AF597251

THE DAILY DECISION OF DELIVERANCE

From Having Authority in the Streets

to Having Authority in the Kingdom

By Kayla A. Crawford

This is a work of nonfiction reflecting the author's personal faith journey.

Photographs and cover design by Kayla Crawford. Background image created using Canva.com.

For more information about the author and her ministry, visit www.KaylaCrawford.com

ISBN: [979-8-234-01656-0]

First Edition, 2026

Printed in the United States of America

Table of Contents

Acknowledgements

Above all, Lord God, thank You for being the head of my life. Thank You for pulling me out of dark places. Thank You for forgiving my dirty sin. Thank You for not exposing all my dirt. Thank You for covering me in times when I made my bed in hell. And Thank You for Your Spirit that lives on the inside of me.

To my Pastors, JJ Hairston and Trina Hairston: thank you for accepting this assignment to be shepherds to some hungry people and for being so understanding of one's lifestyle. I truly believe the Lord led me to your church not because we look alike physically, but because we look alike spiritually. Because of your ministry, I've been able to spiritually grow, walk in my purpose, and receive the promises God has over my life. Thank you for not only being my Pastors, but my Spiritual Parents.

To Prophetess Sharon Roach: thank you for speaking life into me from the very day we met. I believe the Lord strategically allowed our paths to cross so you could walk with me throughout my deliverance. After receiving deliverance at my church, you stood by my side daily—from early morning prayer calls to simply listening as I processed everything.

I am grateful for my family, friends, and prayer partners who encouraged me and stood with me throughout this journey.

My prayer is that this testimony brings hope, healing, and freedom to all who read it.

Who Should Read This Book

Are you ready for something new? I was ready to truly walk in my calling, but I had no idea how to get free from my lifestyle. I didn't know that true freedom could only come from the Lord.

If you are struggling with the lifestyle I once lived—selling drugs, partying, cussing, or fighting—this book is for you. If you are dealing with addictions like drinking, smoking, fornication, or worse, this book is for you.

If you've struggled to find your place in life, searching for your "tribe" or for people who truly appreciate you for who you are, this book is for you. I know what it's like to feel different and to long for acceptance, yet still wonder who genuinely has your best interest at heart.

If you are currently incarcerated, or have been in the past, this book is especially for you.

This book is also for ministries, leaders, and anyone helping others overcome life's struggles—my testimony shows that if God could do this for me, He can do it for anyone. It can serve as a guide to navigate the journey from a treacherous lifestyle into a holy, victorious life.

Are you ready to be delivered and walk in your salvation? This book exists to remind you that God sees you, no matter your circumstances. It is designed to build your faith, strengthen your walk with Him, and show that every addiction, bondage, and stronghold can be overcome through the power of the Holy Spirit.

Whether you are just beginning your journey to freedom or have already been delivered and need encouragement to stay faithful, this book is for you.

Chapter 1

THE STREETS DONT OWE ME NOTHING

People look at my lifestyle and say, *"I still smoke, I'm not where you are. I still drink; I'm not at your level yet."* And that's okay. Deliverance doesn't happen overnight. It takes time, and once you are free of strongholds, you must choose if freedom is something you will keep. I didn't come to church seeking deliverance; I came seeking a relationship with God, knowing I needed Him in my life. In His perfect timing, He delivered me, setting me free from a reckless lifestyle I had carried since childhood. I had been yearning for a way out of the life I had built for myself. I never wanted to spend my life smoking, drinking, and partying every single day, but that was all I had ever known.

I was born in Landover, Maryland, just outside of Washington, D.C., and my life has unfolded across the DMV. I lived in Anne Arundel County, Prince George's County, and Washington, D.C. Growing up, I went to go-go's and loved being outside—fighting, going to clubs, and attending house parties at a young age. I had good parents who did the best they could. Though we didn't have everything, we had enough to survive. My parents didn't raise me in the streets, yet I was drawn to them. I ran to the street's day in and day out. Molded by the world around me, I became a product of my environment. I believe it all began simply by going outside as a child, around the age of eight or nine. Back in the early 2000s, it was just me and my older sister playing outside with no parental guidance. My parents trusted us to return home when the streetlights came on, not knowing that I was already learning how to navigate the streets. I come from a Black family with both my parents in the home, and they knew how to make it look good, even when it wasn't all good. I grew up in a two-bedroom apartment: my parents had a room, and my older sister and I shared one. At first, we shared a twin bed, then moved to bunk beds, and eventually each had our own separate twin bed.

My father passed away when I was in ninth grade. He and my mother had been married for nineteen years, and he died on September 19, 2009—which is the same date they had gotten married in 1992. I looked at it as a book once opened, now closed. My father earned most of the money in our household, so when he passed, the responsibility fell on my mother to care for my sister and me on her own. She always had a job and was intelligent, knowing how to make the most of life with the little we had. My father had put us in a house before he died, but after his passing, my mother struggled to keep up with it all—yet God always made a way. My sister started working at Popeyes to support herself. I was only fourteen, so I couldn't get an official job yet, but at the age of fifteen I found babysitting gigs around the area and earned money watching other people's children. When I turned sixteen, I got my first job at Potbelly Sandwich Shop. I worked there for two years and left at eighteen after I was fired. I was fired for repeatedly arriving late to my shifts. Yet within those two years, I met my first love. At that time, we both attended Meade High School in Maryland and began dating when I was seventeen. After graduation, we spent our days and nights roaming the streets together. He lived in Northeast D.C., and I often stayed with him, despite my job being thirty minutes away.

Transportation issues led to repeated late arrivals, and the unreliability of the metro when traveling out Maryland eventually resulted in my termination. Getting fired didn't faze me. I had grown up stealing whatever I wanted and knew how to survive on my own. I relied on public transportation or rides to shopping malls, not to shop, but to steal clothes and shoes for myself. At one point, everything in my wardrobe was stolen. My clothes were stylish, the kind that turned heads—but I hadn't paid for a single piece, except for my shoes, which were a little more difficult to steal. I started stealing things around the age of fourteen.

School was never easy for me. I struggled with behavior problems. In eighth grade alone, I was suspended eight times, which led to me being kicked out. High school didn't slow me down; I got suspended about fifteen times for fighting, skipping class, and causing disruptions.

I was on the verge of getting kicked out of high school. The final straw came when I got into a big fight, and the school finally kicked me out. My mother tried to enroll me in another high school, but they wouldn't accept me because of my behavior history. She returned to the original school week after week, begging them to take me back. After 90 days of being kicked out, they allowed it—on one condition: I had to sign a contract promising not to get into any more trouble, and then they would allow me to come back.

During those 90 days at home, not enrolled in school, my mother refused to let me sit around without being productive. She told me to call my job at Potbelly Sandwich Shop and get on the daytime schedule. So, at the age of sixteen while everyone else was in school, I was at work, making money. I saw my first $1,000 legally, and once I got a taste of that, I never wanted to stop making money.

About two years later, my same boyfriend ended up taking my virginity. I ended up becoming pregnant in 2014 at the age of eighteen but had an abortion. Getting threatened to be kicked out of the house for being pregnant, I knew I would have to stay with my boyfriend, but his house was really trapped out and roach infested. Honestly, I wasn't ready to have a baby anyway, so I got an abortion.

A year later, at the age of nineteen, I began going to jail for stealing, DUIs, and DWIs (driving under the influence while underage). I was sentenced to three years of supervised probation, yet even then, I kept finding myself behind bars again and again. Over the next six years, I ended up locked up about seven times in total. In 2015, I violated my probation by getting arrested twice within a few months, which led to a sentence at Prince George's County Correctional Facility in Upper Marlboro, Maryland, where I spent several months behind bars. I didn't care much about risking my freedom. I would come home from being incarcerated, only to get locked up again a few weeks later. I remember the correctional officer at Prince George's County Correctional Facility asking me, *"What are you doing back here?"* I know an angel of the Lord walked with me, because many things that should have kept me in jail for longer, didn't. There are countless things I did in the streets that should have landed me behind bars—or worse, I should've been dead.

Before I was sentenced to jailtime, I had to appear before my probation judge. He was a stern Black man, and I thought maybe he'd cut me some slack—but he didn't care about my age, my background, or anything else. He was all about teaching young people a lesson. Being on probation, I had to come visit him in court whenever I got in illegal trouble, so he knew exactly who I was and was familiar with my repeated history. At this particular time, I had violated my probation twice. When my case was called, the officers brought me from the back of the courtroom in handcuffs. I stood before the judge as he said, *"Miss Crawford, I've given you many chances. This time, there is no bond. You'll return in a few months for another court date."* I couldn't believe what I was hearing. Even the people in the courtroom murmured in surprise. Furious, I stormed off in my handcuffs, kicking the door open with my feet as I marched out. I didn't even give the judge a chance to dismiss me—I was too angry to wait.

During those three months in jail, the showers were always cold, there was never any hot water. We had to wait our turn, often showering after someone else, which wasn't sanitary. People would try to walk into your cell to steal your food while you weren't there. I became the lookout for my cellmate, who would take food from other inmates' cells. The correctional officers were always harsh and seemed to dislike me, saying they had heard about me. I couldn't talk to my family or friends because they didn't have money on their phones, though my mother and sister would visit from time to time.

After being released, I continued taking risks that could have landed me back in jail—but the Lord protected me. While locked up, I spent more time in my faith than ever before, because there was nothing else to do and no distractions around. The jail would bring in churches to hold services in the unit, and at the time, I didn't realize that those were little seeds being planted in me—seeds that have blossomed into the faith I have today. I would attend every church service, even if it meant going three times a day, because I would do anything to get out of my cell. Sometimes I lied just to escape—saying I was in pain so I could visit the nurse or claiming I had a child so I could take the parental class. Court dates became another way out; riding the jail bus to the courtroom down the street gave me even more time outside my cell, and honestly, I preferred that ride over anything else, hoping I would see people I knew in the courtroom since I was well known in the area.

Even while incarcerated, I continued my education. I took a nail tech and cosmetology class offered at the jail, and I still have the certification of completion to this day. Despite everything, I actually had fun at Prince George's County Correctional Facility. But not every jail is the same. Immediately after being released from Prince George's, I couldn't go home—an open warrant awaited me in Fairfax County, Virginia from a "burglary tools" charge. Officials transported me directly from Prince George's to Fairfax County Jail in Alexandria, Virginia where I spent an extra week waiting on bail. That week felt like a month. A correctional officer immediately put me in solitary confinement for "catching an attitude," and I spent the time in a small cell, away from everyone. I was used to solitary confinement by then, because I experienced it before in the previous jail, but it still tested my patience.

When I finally came home from that process, I told myself I was done with jail for good. I believed that chapter of my life was over. But five years later, in 2020, I was arrested again at the Fifth District Police Station in Washington, D.C., on an assault charge. I was released a few hours later, and this time, I knew—without doubt—that it truly was my last time.

Over the years as I grew older, I spent eight years selling drugs—until the day I was delivered at my church in 2024. I sold molly, weed, and Percocet, or "percs." I started selling molly in 2015, a season of my life that I remember clearly. I had just come home from being incarcerated, and my criminal record made it nearly impossible to get a job. Even Target denied me. I eventually found work in a warehouse office, the only company willing to hire me. I made $12 an hour, which in 2015 that was manageable. Slow money is better than no money, so I took the job, working forty hours a week. But even then, I found myself turning back to the streets.

One day during my lunch break, I drove over to the carryout to grab something to eat. A man started talking to me and, judging by how I looked and dressed, he could tell I was in the streets. He offered me a chance to sell drugs for him—molly, to be exact. He said he would front me a 3.5 of molly, which could bring in hundreds of dollars in profit if I sold it. In that moment, I realized I had just met the "plug." That was the moment I agreed to enter the drug world with him. From then on, I met him near his home—he never let me go to his actual house. I had to bring back a portion of the money but I still made a significant profit for myself. That was the start of my hustle. I saw it as a miracle, finally making money outside of a job that paid only twelve dollars an hour. That job eventually came to an end, and soon selling drugs became my only source of income. Once I accepted that this was how I was surviving, I went out and bought a gun and a trap phone (a disposable phone). In 2016, at twenty-one years old, I purchased my first handgun, a .22, a deuce-deuce. I knew people could be plotting against me, so I carried it every time I left the house. I never left it behind. Just like a cell phone you take everywhere, that's how I kept my gun—always on me.

One day, I lost contact with my molly plug—his number stopped working, and I never heard from him again. I had to find other molly suppliers, though I didn't want too. My clients had always said my molly was pure and strong, and I didn't want to compromise that reputation. Molly is a mix of substances—ecstasy, meth, and sometimes people say PCP. I never knew exactly what was in it. All I knew was the effect it had on me, how it used to have me high as a kite. Now in the process of finding another drug dealer, I was afraid that the quality of the product wouldn't be as good. Once I found new plugs, I began distributing molly again. But I eventually stopped—mostly because I realized I didn't truly know what was in it, and I didn't want to unknowingly kill anyone, especially with fentanyl becoming so common. I sold molly for about three years, finally stopping around 2019. I was taking it myself, and it became an addiction. Selling it made it far too accessible. I would crumble molly into my weed before rolling it—what we called a "boot jay." Sometimes, I'd drop it into Hennessy bottles so I could get drunk and high at the same time. I lost a lot of weight; at one point, I was almost a toothpick. The drug suppresses appetite, but I had taken it so often that my body adjusted, and I could still eat. Looking back, I'm so grateful to know that the Lord protected me throughout my addictions and my life in the streets.

Drinking hard liquor like Hennessy, smoking weed, and taking molly became my favorite combination. It had me fried, and for a while, it eased my pain. I got used to enjoying life this way, not realizing how much it was controlling me. I had planned to stop taking molly when my close friend Keyonna Kilette—whom we called "Keshay"—passed away. One night, we were all out celebrating my birthday and another mutual friend's birthday. The day was filled with drinking and smoking, and we ended up having a small birthday party for us. I left early, needing to take three people home and be up early for work the next morning.

Keshay stayed behind, still turning up with our other friends. Around 1:00 a.m., she texted to check on me. I replied that I was home and fine, then I asked if she was okay—but she never responded. Around 8:00 a.m., I received a call that would change everything: she had passed away. It was the morning of September 7th, 2016. I immediately left work and went to her house, wanting to see if what I heard was true.

At the time, I was working at the UPS Store in Laurel, MD, and Keshay lived in Bowie, MD, so it didn't take long for me to get to her house. When I arrived, her dad opened the door, and I learned she had been in a car accident on her way home around 5:00 a.m., just off Route 50 at the 197 Collington Road exit. She was literally almost home. Her car hit a tree and caught fire. She was trapped and burned to death. Her family told me that the fire was so intense, the police had to identify her with her tooth. The news crushed me. I cried for months. I had just seen her hours before. It shook me deeply because we were always careful drivers—even when we were drunk. She used to always pick me up way before I even had my first car, so I knew firsthand how skilled she was behind the wheel. She was like my street twin. We knew our way around these DC streets, and the thought of her being gone so suddenly was so unbearable.

We knew everybody and had a certain type of respect that we demanded, always having each other's back. I knew she was drunk because that morning I went to watch her stories on social media and saw her swerving the car around 4:45 a.m., shortly before the accident. Sometimes, I can't help but feel like it should've been me.

After she died, I faced attacks from a group of her friends that I barely knew—people I rarely saw her hang out with. They blamed her death on me, saying it was my fault because it was my birthday, and that I was the last person to see her—even though our other friends from the party were still with her. I kept thinking that if I had stayed longer, I would have been able to make sure she didn't drive back drunk. I was trying to process the grief of losing someone I called my sister. She was the realest friend I ever had. Even to this day, I haven't met anyone as genuine as her. A lot of women say they're real, but underneath, they're filled with hatred, envy, and jealousy. They ain't got no loyalty, and they don't understand the street code. They get intimidated by the love people give you—or by the respect dudes show you, a respect they haven't earned for themselves. Females wanted what I had. They envied how I paved a way for myself and financially supported myself. But I never understood that—we all get the same 24 hours to get up and get it. It wasn't my fault they didn't decide to go get the money. But I realized it's *in* you, not *on* you, and real is rare. Dealing with females in the streets was not easy. But Keshay was not like that—She was thoroughbred, cut from a completely different cloth. We always saw eye to eye. Our hustle, our grind and our lifestyle was always alike. Dealing with the backlash from her old friends got so messy that we ended up having separate candlelight's just to celebrate her. Coming together as one? Forget it.

It felt like our whole friend circle against her old friend circle. We were so close to throwing hands at her candlelight vigil—and even at the funeral. It was straight-up ghetto. But this death hit me hard. Right after my birthday, I must celebrate my friend's death.

I believe the Lord showed me what happened to her. I was always wondering how that accident happened. The 197 exit is wide. Spacious. It's not a ramp, not a curvy road—just a straight shot that bares off to the right, with a stoplight. So, I kept thinking... what could've caused her car to crash into that tree? After she passed, I told myself I'd slow down. Stop turning up. Stop going out. That didn't happen. I kept moving like nothing had changed. A month later, late at night—two or three in the morning, I took the exit to my house. (Just like Keshay). Minutes later... I ran into the back of someone's truck. I was almost home. I don't know how it happened. One moment I was awake. The next... it was too late. Sleep had taken over me. The crash hit hard—so hard it woke me back up. I thought for sure someone would get out of the car. But they didn't. Instead, they sped off, like fear pushed their foot on the gas. Behold, I felt the tangible presence of someone sitting in the passenger seat. I kept looking to my right because I *knew* someone was there—but of course, I saw no one. In that moment, I realized it was an angel. I didn't have the words to explain what I was feeling; I only knew it was supernatural. Right after that, I felt that was the Lord was showing me the truth—what happened to Keshay that night. She fell asleep at the wheel. After that, instead of me slowing down, I numbed myself. I used molly to keep going through the pain, through the grief. I kept selling it. I kept using weed, and getting drunk, even when I should've stopped.

I had a feeling my mother knew I was selling drugs. I always had money, even though she knew I couldn't work because of my criminal background. I'd show her a stack of cash, and she'd be so proud of me—never questioning where it came from. She just knew I was taking care of myself, being independent, and making a way. She loved that about me.

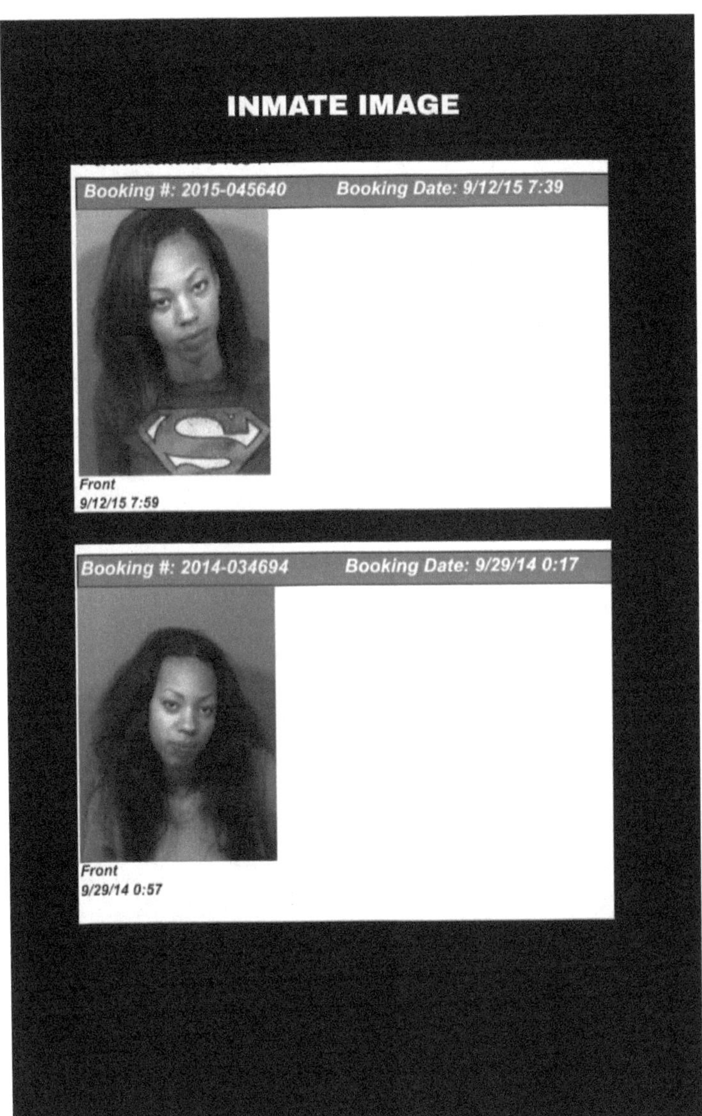
INMATE IMAGE
Booking #: 2015-045640
Booking Date: 9/12/15 7:39
Front
9/12/15 7:59
Booking #: 2014-034694
Booking Date: 9/29/14 0:17
Front
9/29/14 0:57

REST IN PEACE DADDY

REST IN PEACE
KEYONNA KILLETTE "KESHAY"
KILLETTE
KEYONNA S.
JUNE 21, 1993
SEPT. 7, 2016

Chapter 2

ITS A DAILY DECISION TO STAY DELIVERED

Fast forward to 2020—that was the year I learned how to scam for a living. What I once tried to justify as a hustle was really theft. I was taking money that didn't belong to me, knowing deep down that what I was doing was wrong, but I didn't care because the money was coming in so fast. Through the dark web, I had access to people's banking information from all over the world, different countries, states and cities. All I had to do was purchase their banking information with cryptocurrency. I chose a gas station I felt I could return to without drawing attention, one that had a Bitcoin machine inside. The bitcoin machine was important because I would bring cash and convert it into cryptocurrency, then send that Bitcoin to a wallet I used on the dark web. From there, I used cryptocurrency to buy stolen banking information, believing that using Bitcoin instead of my personal card would keep everything from being traced back to me. I was fully aware that what I was doing was wrong. I used the money to treat myself, taking myself out to some of the fanciest restaurants—places like Del Frisco's, Ruth's Chris, Benihana's, and many others. I moved through high-end spots in Washington, D.C., as if nothing could touch me. The Cheesecake Factory became my go-to, until they eventually caught on and started blocking my number. I realized it wasn't the number they were blocking, they blocked my phone from its IP Address, but a true scammer never has just one phone. I had about 4-5 phones, so I could keep going.

With the bank information I had access to, I started making money by offering to pay people's bills for half of what they owed. They would send me half of the bill owed, and I used stolen banking information to cover the bill. I also used stolen banking information to order liquor online. When it was delivered to my house, I sold the liquor bottles at nighttime, after hours, for discounted prices, basically running a small liquor operation. I even paid thousands of dollars on car tickets. I paid for one of my friend's tickets and it went through, but when I paid that same friend's phone bill, it triggered an alert and backfired on their account. After that, I stopped paying bills with stolen card information, but I didn't stop scamming. I still had other methods going. I didn't just have scam hustles—I also ran a legal business selling Funnel, which is a type of tobacco leaf called Fronto, used to smoke with your weed. My Funnel business was booming. Everyone loved it; I had the best Funnel in the city. It grew across the DMV area, and I eventually got my product into 30 stores, including Shell and Exxon gas stations, corner stores, liquor stores, and more. I went into one of my corner stores that sold my product and made $450 in a single transaction just by selling my Funnel, which the store would then resell for a profit. My product, called Lachena's Funnel, can still be found on Instagram today. I closed the business in 2024 after giving my life to Christ. Even though it was a legal way to make fast money, I knew it would interfere with my walk with Jesus.

I learned how to scam by meeting some people in Bronx, New York. My dad is from the Bronx, so I would go there time to time visiting my grandmother. She passed away from COVID in 2020. Rest in peace to my grandmother, she was a legend in her state. Back in the 80s, she built a park for kids in the Bronx called "Alpha Crawford Sunshine Park." The park has been demolished, but its history can still be found online. At that time, I drove out to see my grandmother's gravesite and to get my Funnel products into stores in New York City. I was excited about selling my Funnel there because I knew it would bring in more money and make me feel like I was doing big things having it in a different state. I went out there with the intention of getting new stores as clients for my business. While I was there, I met some people who were scammers. This particular night, I was outside hanging out with them, and I was nervous because I was by myself and didn't have my gun on me. The Bronx trenches are very different from what I was used to in DC. One of the guys I met showed me how to scam. That was the day I officially became a scammer, and I knew I was going to take what I learned back home and use it. When I got back home, I started setting up shop and promoting my scamming lifestyle. As time went on, I continued living a life of sin—scamming, partying, and fornicating.

In 2021, I had sexual relations with someone I was doing scams with, and I ended up getting pregnant. I was so mad at myself for getting pregnant again, especially since six months earlier, in 2020, I just had an abortion. The second pregnancy involved a guy in my neighborhood off Minnesota Ave in Washington, D.C. It started with me just buying weed from him, and then I became pregnant. Fast forward six months later, and here I was, pregnant again for the third time. One day I realized something didn't feel right, so I went downtown to George Washington Hospital to get tested for STDs, and they also ran a pregnancy test. My mother used to work at that hospital, so I often went to their emergency room. The results came back: I had an STD and I was pregnant. I couldn't believe it. They gave me pills to treat the STD, while I tried to process what to do next with this pregnancy, knowing I had just had an abortion six months ago.

I decided to go to my abortion clinic downtown—it's pitiful to know that I even had an abortion clinic that knew of me in the first place. When I got there, they asked me, *"What are you doing back here?"* It was so embarrassing to be back at the same clinic for the same reason just six months later. I didn't tell anyone I was pregnant except for a close friend. I went through the abortion process on my own, too embarrassed to admit I was on my third abortion at the age of 25. At that time, I thought having abortions was fine because that was the only solution I knew when I didn't want a baby.

Back to scamming—one day, my friend TB, who lived down the street from me, got involved with my lifestyle. We were very close. We hung out almost every day. He knew I was a scammer and let me borrow a card-making machine. (TB was later murdered in his own neighborhood in Southeast, DC called *"19th & Minnesota"* in 2022.) This card-making machine he let me use, allowed me to be able to take a blank card and transfer your online credentials to the physical card I was creating, so in stores whenever I swiped the new card, I programmed it to pull information off the stolen bank card. Lord knows, once I surrendered my life to Christ, I asked for forgiveness for doing such horrible things. At that time, my mind was just set on survival mode. Another scam I did that brought in a lot of money involved stealing funds from the federal government in various amounts. One of my partners in scamming had access to checks, and we took the chance when opportunities came up. I knew the risk—if I got caught, I would be prosecuted for fraud which could ruin my career path for life. We deposited stolen business checks into bank accounts, some of them worth several thousand dollars. I was aware that larger deposits could trigger attention, and I didn't want any red flags tied back to me. That year, I made over

$100,000 from fraudulent checks but I had to split the money with my scamming partner.

In 2023, I finally stopped scamming after I felt a strong pull in my spirit to stop. I believe that was the Lord protecting me from what could have happened. But one day, I did something involving my mom. She had no idea. I knew she was struggling—she was about nine months behind on her car payments and owed around $3,300. I had cosigned for the car, so the missed payments were hurting my credit too, and the car was up for being repossessed. At the same time, she was dealing with homelessness and had lost her apartment. I didn't think she would be able to catch up anytime soon. I felt bad that she didn't have a job or house, and I didn't want her to lose her car. So, I called my scamming partner, and we bussed a check that week, which covered the $3,300 she owed on her car payment. She was so happy, and I felt good that I could help her, even though she didn't know that this was fraudulent money. After that, I really stopped and decided I was done with scamming. When I officially stopped scamming, I went back to selling weed. I was spending so much money on smoking that I thought selling it could help me save money. I loved weed—I had been smoking just about every day since I was sixteen. I turned to it for healing, for happiness, when I was sad, and even just out of boredom. Technically, I had made weed an idol. I tried my best to quit in 2024, but it was almost impossible because I was so addicted. I reached a point in my life where I said, *"Lord, I'm ready for a new life. I want to slow down on smoking."* I gave it my all to try my best to stop, but it never worked. When I finally experienced deliverance in April 2024 at my church, I realized the truth: I couldn't do it on my own—I had to do it with Jesus.

On April 11th, 2024, I was delivered at my church. It was my first time actually being apart of a church and showing up consistently as a member. I had been going there on and off for about a year—I found it on TikTok. I had typed in 'Black Churches in DC' because something inside me was pulling me to be in church. Growing up, me and my mother only went to church on special occasions—I didn't really know what it meant to have a relationship with God, but I always believed in Him. I never heard of the Holy Spirit, I never heard of speaking in tongues, and I defiantly never been down to an altar before, so this was all new for me. But a year after I started attending this church, everything changed. On the day of my deliverance, the Lord broke every chain that had bound me for so long. He tore down the strongholds and pulled me out of a lifestyle that had left me empty and broken. For the first time, I felt the weight lift, And I tasted the freedom and peace, that flows from living a life that truly pleases Him.

I always came into church sitting in the last row of the sanctuary, that was my comfort zone—I didn't want anyone to notice me. I just wanted to be in the house of the Lord, unnoticed and hidden. I wanted to hide... but of course, you can't hide from God. I had been going to this church for a year, but that particular day was different. It was the day the Lord called me out of hiding—the day I experienced a supernatural encounter with God for the very first time. I had never heard of a minister. I barely knew any gospel music, and I had never even spoken to a pastor before. Everything about this church was completely new to me.

My pastor, Trina Hairston, called me out from the back. The Lord had highlighted me to her, and the moment she prophesied over my life, I broke into deliverance. I believe that was the moment I was filled with the Holy Spirit. I couldn't believe the Lord had noticed me—and chosen me. When I got home, I gave away all my weed and threw out all my liquor. I knew this was my escape route to a new life. Just a few days before this happened, after a Sunday service, I heard the Lord say, *"Get ready."* It was the very first time I had ever heard God speak to me. So, when my deliverance happened at church, all I could think about were those words. At the time, I didn't understand it fully, but God was telling me to get ready for a completely new life—a life I never could have imagined on my own.

Now, I make a daily decision to stay delivered. Every morning when I wake up, I choose to walk in my freedom. I choose to stay free. Even though I'm no longer bound by strongholds, I face them every day. I see the same people still trapped in the lifestyle I left behind. I see the same friends I grew up with, doing things I can no longer participate in. Walking in deliverance means choosing every day to not go back to my old life, even when the old habits are all around me. I used to have a very bad temper; it didn't take much for me to get angry. But the Lord delivered me from it all, and today, I don't look like the person I used to be. Even in the midst of my sin, God graciously had a plan for me. I was hurt growing up, carrying the weight of all the trauma around me and in my household. I have many scar wounds from those experiences. For a while, I found myself alone, searching in the streets for the love I was missing. But now I understand that all I ever needed was to fully find Jesus. After receiving deliverance, it's my choice whether I stay set apart or get caught up in worldly activities again. Honestly, living a sinful life is so much easier, it's comfortable and familiar. Walking as a believer of Christ is harder, but it's where true freedom and purpose are found.

It's easier to live a sinful life because that's the only lifestyle that I knew. Now all a sudden I have to live this Holy lifestyle that I don't even know how to do. I literally depend on the Lord for my strength. He is my Master Teacher, guiding me every day on how to live right. Without Him, I know I would fall back into my old ways. I was willing to make this decision because I knew it would bring me a step closer to a fresh start. For the first time, I could finally breathe—the chains were broken.

REST IN PEACE GRANDMA

Chapter 3

SOMETIMES I GRIEVE MY OLD LIFE

I make a daily decision to stay delivered. I grieve my old life—not because I want to return to it, but because I laid my whole life down for Christ. As I spent time with drug dealers, street superstars, and murderers, I found myself slowly becoming one of them. The street credibility I gained made me known around town. People recognized me, respected me, and defended me—often in ways that were dangerous. I was considered 'one of the men,' even though I was female. Out here in the streets, I was a rare breed—often called the last of a dying breed. When you're street-smart, you can peep a rare one, the kind of person that doesn't come around easily. This is what allowed me to gain favor with others. I would come outside with fresh shoes, my hair and nails done, and colorful lipstick.

Depending on my outfit, it gave me a certain look that let others sense my rareness. I believe I inherited this rareness from my father—since he grew up in the streets, I took after him very well. My street smarts also gave me another level of what we call discernment. Even though I never intended to murder anyone, running the streets made me realize it could go that way. I started to develop a 'stack or starve' mindset. Over the years, from childhood into adulthood, I accumulated haters—people who always had something to say about me or my success. I got used to it; it became normal. Once I realized I had gained favor in the streets with men, I felt like the streets were mine! Like I had the keys. But in reality, I was using a God-given gift for the wrong purpose. That type of influence was meant to bring encouragement and change lives for Christ, not to make me part of the statistics.

Many of us use the gifts given from Heaven for worldly purposes, not realizing they come from above. Too often, we find ourselves cultivating these gifts for selfish desires. But now, I refuse to allow my gift to be contaminated! It will no longer be used for the world—it will be used for Heavenly purposes. My mother told me I have the "gift of gab" which is the ability to speak well and persuade others. It made sense, because in the streets I knew how to sell my drugs to talk in a way that got me what I needed. Now, I use that same ability to share the Gospel, reaching non-believers so they can become followers of Christ.

Sometimes I feel pain when friends and family pass away. Other times, I feel pain by just sitting and grieving my old life. I miss it—not because I wanna go back, but cause the streets were all I knew. I ended up laying it all down to follow Jesus. I had fun in my sin—smoking weed, hitting the clubs, selling drugs, and throwing hands whenever I felt disrespected. Yeah, it was kinda fun. Scamming and getting whatever I wanted without using my own money? That was fun. But it wasn't the will of God for me. Sometimes I catch myself missing the world—I'm only human. But I know what the Lord has for me is bigger than anything out there. That's why I must choose every day to stay delivered.

How do you live one lifestyle your whole life, then suddenly start a new one that you got to learn from scratch? Of course I miss what I got free from! That's why some people, even after being delivered, end up going back—the weight of the streets feels more familiar than the freedom in Christ. Yeah, I might grieve my old life sometimes, but I can't look back. I laid my whole life down for Christ. If I tried going back, the enemy would be ready to trap me—or even take my life. He hates the children of the light, especially those with an assignment over their lives.

Building a real relationship with God has been everything for me. When I grieve my old life, I remind myself of the Father—His love outweighs every temptation the world throws at me. Would I go back, disappoint God, and risk losing my assignment? Or move forward in Him and let Him use me for Kingdom works?

Your deliverance ain't just for you! It's for the people around you; the souls you're giving hope to. When I realized how many lives were tied to my testimony, I knew I couldn't go back. I even vented to a friend one day, telling her I can't afford to mess up. She said, 'God's grace is sufficient, so even if you do, He'll understand.' She's right, but that wasn't my situation. If I go back, so many souls depending on me would give up if I gave up. Some people already think it's okay to have one foot in the world and one foot out, but I can't live like that. I need people around me who are solid in their walk, who ain't halfway in the world. Coming out of that life, it's triggering for me to be around folks still living in it. Some people won't get it, but when God is doing a new thing in your life, you got to be around people headed where you're going—or already there. I don't need anything reminding me too much of my past, cause that can be a trigger leading straight back into temptation—especially when I'm grieving my old lifestyle. That's why, after surrendering my life to Christ, I've learned I got to protect my salvation. I can't move the same way I did before. I can't show up to certain places anymore. As I protect my salvation, I'm still grieving my life before Christ. Going through old pictures, seeing how lit I was... yeah, I get taken back to the fun moments in the streets. But even through that grief of my old lifestyle, I choose to maintain my salvation. I ain't going back.

When I'm out running an errand late at night and I run into a group of people who are lit and having fun, it sometimes makes me think about how much fun I used to have living in sin and being lost. When I hear people asking to buy 'funnel for their weed' in the stores, I think about how I used to go to each person and tell them about my funnel business that I had and sold it in different stores. Even though I closed that business once I got delivered, I still get taken back to the days when I was in business. Enjoying the world and everything it has to offer was so much fun, and sometimes I miss it because I spent 28 years living that lifestyle. This is where temptation comes in and can make people feel like they can't be free or that they might backslide. This is when you must make a daily decision to stay delivered. If you've lived the lifestyle I lived—fast money, illegal money, drugs, sex, and guns as the way you survived in childhood and adulthood—then I know firsthand exactly what you struggle with.

When you want to stay pure before God, but your flesh smells the weed in your neighborhood while walking down the street—and that one smell brings up a flood of memories from the lifestyle you gave up—what do you do when that one smell tests your salvation? It's not easy being a child of God when you come out of a street full of sin. For some of us, living holy has been one of the hardest things to do. It was easier going out to sell drugs and getting locked up. At least I knew how to thug that lifestyle out.

This whole new life I'm living? I've never lived this before. It's the opposite of what I know—something completely new in my adult life. I literally have to unlearn my old ways of living and learn new ways of living that are holy and acceptable to Christ. It's hard not to cuss somebody out. It's hard not to put your hands on somebody who disrespects you right in front of your face. It's hard to depend on God to provide when you're used to getting illegal fast cash. God help me. Have mercy on us. Whenever these thoughts come up, I have to remind myself that the world was just a temporary feeling of fun. Then, over time, my old toxic ways of thinking start to change to what would Jesus do?

When experiencing these feelings, I command myself to push through. Pushing through for me often comes through praise and worship. My deliverance pushed forth my praise. There are times I don't feel like lifting my hands or dancing, but I force myself to, letting the devil know he can't shut me up. Sometimes I don't feel like opening my mouth to bless the Lord, but for my life, it's got to be done. Once I understood the power in my 'YES,' I never let myself say 'NO.' I command my soul to bless the Lord at all times! There's power in the pressing. Your breakthrough might be on the line. It's the pressing and the crushing that's going to produce the fruit in your life. An olive got to be pressed to make oil. Grapes got to be pressed to make new wine. And when a seed is planted, it needs water to grow. Watering is a good nutritious way—but what about when it rains? Storms come, but even in the storm, the rain hits that seed, still helping it grow. You're still growing in the middle of the storm. You're still producing fruit in your rainy season. You might've wanted to just be watered, but you can't control the storm. It comes and goes when it wants. You got to endure your rainy season, keep pressing, and know that fruit is still coming out of you, even though the storm. There have been plenty of days when I felt like giving up. I grew up with little to no support system anyway. Nobody was pushing me to bless the Lord. Back then, when I needed healing, I pushed myself to roll up weed. When I needed to feel numb, I drank liquor. I knew how to push myself to feel better by not being sober. Now I understand—that same push is what I must apply to keep going forward in God, even when I don't feel like it. Life hasn't been easy. I never dealt with suicidal thoughts, and I thank God for that, but giving up crossed my mind many times. But the winner in me refused to quit, so instead, I ran to drugs and alcohol to numb the pain that I didn't want to face. I don't push through because I want to—I push through because I have to. The enemy is waiting to catch me slipping. Every day, I push through to wake up with a positive attitude, to change my language, to speak life and not death. I push through to keep curse words from leaving my mouth in times of stress. I push through to trust God even when I don't know what that looks like for me.

I've had my own apartment for 8 years, and in that time, I've gone through seasons with no job or money to cover bills. Still, I trusted God to provide. Grieving my old lifestyle makes me think about all the fast cash I used to touch whenever it was a dry season I had access to a quick come up, illegally. However, being in Christ that is not an option for me. I must push through, because if I don't, I could miss a mark–maybe for myself, or maybe for someone else to be set free. Quitting could shake someone else's faith. If I had given up, people might not have wanted to give their lives to Christ. That's why I stay clear of distractions. When I start reminiscing about the past, I remind myself it was temporary fun. That fun didn't hold weight like being in Christ. I must remind myself: don't look back too long, keep your eyes on the road ahead. When temptation hits, I ask: why would I risk my relationship with Jesus for a temporarily worldly desire?

Chapter 4

WITHSTAND THE EVIL DAY

Two weeks after I was delivered from the streets, in April 2024, I took a shared ride home. That ride proved to me that the reality of the unseen world that the Bible speaks about is very real. Being freshly set free from the world and the enemy's camp, I realized I had just experienced my first real encounter with the devil. One early afternoon after getting off my government job, I ordered a shared-ride home because I didn't feel like riding the train. I was on the phone with a family friend when the car arrived, and I got in still talking. The car was empty at first, but because it was a shared ride, the driver later stopped to pick up another passenger. When we pulled up to pick up the other passenger, I got a bad vibe—her face expression looked off. She got in, and I asked how she was doing. She barely answered, so I went back to my phone call. Then she complimented me, saying my voice was pretty. I thanked her. That's when she tapped the driver and said, "When somebody gives you a compliment, don't you give one back? Well, she ain't say S***!" That's when I knew this ride home was going to be interesting. We had picked her up from a neighborhood called Saratoga on Montana Ave, and I still had about twenty minutes before I'd be home. I didn't respond to what she said to the driver. I knew I had to hold my tongue for those twenty minutes to avoid a confrontation. But staying quiet didn't stop her—she continued to provoke me. She went on to tell me to get off the phone, claiming I was being rude and talking in the driver's ear. I didn't understand what she meant, because none of that was true. That's when I knew she was tripping. Even then, I stayed quiet, holding my tongue and choosing not to respond. I knew I had just been delivered at my church two weeks ago and had started walking in freedom—so I knew this wasn't a random attack, but it was the devil trying me. She ended up calling another girl and started talking about me. Then she got louder on the phone, clearly trying to intimidate me. That's when I finally looked at her and said, 'That doesn't bother me.' She went on to say it was a good day for her to fight somebody because she had just gotten her feet done at the nail salon. None of what she said made sense to me at all. As we were getting close to the 295 highway, she told me I needed to get out of the car and walk. That's when it hit me—I was sitting right next to Satan. I immediately started asking God to help me. While all this was going on, I could see the Uber driver watching me through the rearview mirror, waiting to see how I'd handle it. He never said a word the whole ride. I could tell he was concerned, but he didn't step in. I slowly reached into my pocket and placed my pocket-knife beside my right leg—quietly, without a word. I still didn't say anything to her. For nearly twenty minutes, I sat there in silence while she kept threatening me, talking about how she was going to fight me. As we approached my destination, she told the girl on the phone she was getting herself together to fight before we got out of the car. Then she looked at me and said, 'What?! What you tryna do?' I looked back at her and started laughing. All I could think about was how God had just shown up big in my life two weeks ago—and how hard I was fighting not to react the way I used to. I knew I had a knife on me, and at that moment, I was heated inside. Still, I stayed quiet while she kept provoking me. As we got a few minutes from my house, I texted my neighbor to see if he was home and told him to come downstairs immediately. He asked if he should bring a cart to help with groceries. I told him no—just come now. I chose to text him instead of calling so she wouldn't realize I was making sure someone was there. My neighbor must've already been outside waiting, because he called to ask where I was at. I told him I was pulling up now. I didn't really need help with my bags, but I wanted someone there in case the situation escalated. He ended up calling me because he didn't see the car I was pulling up in and I played it off telling him I needed help with my bags, just because I knew she was listening.

She heard the phone call and saw my neighbor approaching the car. She rolled down her window and yelled at him, "Come help her get her f******g sh*t out the car!" That's when something in me got triggered. Because how dare you come onto my property, to the place where I lay my head, and yell at my neighbor like that? I didn't know her at all, yet she immediately targeted me as soon as she entered the car. I only pulled my knife out to take precautions for self-defense, not with any intention of harming her. I knew I would only react if I were physically attacked. I knew I wasn't dealing with just a person—I was facing something darker—and I chose to remain silent. I had sat there being threatened for nearly twenty minutes, but when she yelled out the window at my neighbor on my property, that crossed the line. I was already stepping out of the car, and at that moment everything escalated fast. Out of anger, I grabbed my knife and stabbed her in the thigh. That's when I looked at her and said, "What you got to say now?" She was in complete shock. She didn't immediately bleed out which let me know she was dehydrated or just completely drunk. That's when the Uber driver hurried up and drove off with her still in the car. I could hear her friend on the phone, still talking while she was in shock. In that moment, I knew the driver had a serious situation on his hands because he had to deal with taking her to the hospital. I knew that eventually she was going to end up bleeding in his car.

Then, I walked inside my building with my neighbor and rubbed her blood off my knife. Once I was finally inside my apartment, everything hit me at once. I broke down, overwhelmed by the reality of what had just happened. At that moment was when I knew that I could potentially be facing some serious legal charges. Just when life started going well for me—I was working a great job, I had just stopped selling drugs and smoking two weeks ago after being delivered at my church, and I was in the middle of leaving my old apartment to move into a better one—reality hit me that I could possibly be throwing my whole life away. I called one of my good men who lived about five to ten minutes away and told him to pull up—it was an emergency. I told him everything that happened, just in case things went left and I needed him to look out for me. After that, fear took over. I went into survival mode, constantly looking over my shoulder. Even when I walked my dog at night, I wasn't at peace—I kept thinking about whether retaliation would come my way, so I kept my gun on me just in case. At the end of the day, she knew where I lived. I stayed in a well-known building in the city—one that was easy to remember.

As soon as I thought I was done with the street life, something tragic happened to me. I felt like the enemy had won and robbed me of the life God had just promised me two weeks ago when my pastor prophesied over my life. Because of this situation, I walked around with my head down, begging God nonstop for forgiveness. I cried out for hours. I kept saying, 'I harmed somebody I was supposed to help.' I asked Him, 'Do You still love me?' and questioned if his love was still there. I felt like the enemy had straight up robbed me of God's blessings. I prayed over the young lady's healing and that she would be okay. Day & night

I repented. I think the enemy wanted to drive me back to weed and liquor, but I didn't let him. It wasn't until I stepped into church the next day, for the Young Adult Bible Study, and that Bible study lifted my head, and I then knew God still loved me. I didn't tell anyone—neither the members nor my pastors' cause I was embarrassed. I was just some girl off the streets, and now I had this tragic story when they were expecting greatness from me. What would they think? So, I kept it private and dealt with it myself. I did tell a family friend, and she encouraged me. I was grateful to have her, because I didn't want to go through this alone. I had my street friends I could've called, but this is a new life for me so I wasn't about to run back to them—I needed someone who could pray for me, because I knew this wasn't just normal, it was spiritual. At this time, I was only two weeks into my surrendered life to Christ, so I didn't know how to put on the 'Full Armor of GOD.'

"Therefore take up the whole armor of God, that you may be able to withstand in the evil day, and having done all, to stand firm. 14 Stand therefore, having fastened on the belt of truth, and having put on the breastplate of righteousness, 15 and, as shoes for your feet, having put on the readiness given by the gospel of peace. 16 In all circumstances take up the shield of

faith, with which you can extinguish all the flaming darts of the evil one; [17] *and take the helmet of salvation, and the sword of the Spirit, which is the word of God,* [18] *praying at all times in the Spirit, with all prayer and supplication. To that end, keep alert with all perseverance, making supplication for all the saints."*

- (Galatians 5:10-18 ESV)

Apostle Paul in the book of Galatians commands us to put on our Full Armor of God and take up the sword of the Spirit, which means to fight the enemy with the Word of God. But at this time, I had no idea how to do so because I hadn't learned it yet on my journey with the Lord; I was only two weeks fresh into this lifestyle. But this was the day I experienced a demon from the unseen world. The devil was angry that I had been freed from his camp and was now walking in the light. So, he tried to send one of his vessels to attack me. The enemy came to rob me of my salvation. He wanted me to throw it all away. We all know the enemy comes to steal, kill, and destroy—but what if he comes to distract you? Distraction is a demonic delay. If he can't pull you out of your character or break you, he'll try to get in your head. If he can get your mind off the assignment God gave you, he wins. In my case, he was trying to distract me from the goodness of God and push me back to a place I had already been healed from. He was trying to steal my salvation. As time went on, the Lord showed me that He still had promises over my life, and I am forever grateful for His grace. I am so glad He forgave me.

See, when you're not living in sin anymore, there's not much to repent for. For those two weeks after deliverance I was living sin-free for the most part. But when I realized I had just stabbed somebody, I repented like never before. That's when I truly understood what it really means to repent for a sin. I stayed in my prayer closet for hours, begging God for forgiveness and praying that this whole situation could bring the young lady to Jesus. I prayed that she'd be delivered and that her thigh would be healed.

This was definitely a demonic distraction for me. Although I learned that some distractions are not all demonic, there are good distractions too—it's important to know the season you're in. Some seasons require extreme focus, and you may not have time to chit-chat like the last season. In the Bible, Abraham had a father named Terah. God told Abraham to leave his father's household and go to a new land called Canaan to inherit the promise. Abraham started the journey, but his father settled in Haran. The name Terah in Hebrew means 'delay.'

Could it be that Abraham's father was a distraction, holding him back from the promise? That may be why God told him to leave. We must check who around us carries the Spirit of Terah. Delay is a form of distraction. Some people may delay us without even meaning to. That's just how they are. This is why we need to discern what voices we allow around us in every season. Some voices can delay us from God's promise. In this hour, it's strategic to make sure you're not influenced by voices that can't see the vision God gave you. It's dangerous to keep a voice in your ear that's not on the same page. One wrong page can throw you off and distract you from hearing what God is saying, just because they're misaligned. It's dangerous to have someone in your ear in a season when they don't understand how God is moving in your life. You've got to separate yourself from distractions—good or bad—so you can reach the place God has shown you. In this case, this was certainly a demonic distraction. However, I was able to overcome it and God's grace showed up for me.

Chapter 5

THE COST OF SALVATION

Whew, child—nobody told me this journey with the Lord would be so emotional. I've lost people, places, and things. But there is not one thing that I lost that the Lord did not restore. Everything I let go of in the name of the Lord; He replaced with so much more. Heaven is keeping an account of your sacrifices. Your sacrifices will never go unnoticed. Salvation requires sacrifice. Walking out true salvation means making lifelong sacrifices. Salvation is more than believing Jesus died on the cross; it includes surrender, deliverance, holiness, and receiving the Holy Spirit. This is a process.

Today, salvation is often half-sold. It's belief without transformation. But we must be reborn in

Christ. Transformation means dying to your old self, putting on your new identity in Christ, and resisting sin. We will all fall short of the glory of God, but that is no excuse to avoid living a set-apart life. Transformation is part of salvation. It costs you your old life, habits, and ways. I became born again by choosing to live a holy life. Holiness is the lifestyle the Lord calls us to live. Living Holy is difficult at first because you must lay down worldly desires. Temptation will come, but you must withstand it and make a daily decision to stay Holy.

My deliverance was essential after salvation because it brought me closer to God. The goal is to be as close to the Lord as possible. Deliverance freed me from strongholds that hindered me from walking in my purpose and deliverance allowed me to be reborn again. It is a beautiful process that unravels us from everything that is not like God. The Lord loves us enough to set us free from any addiction, lust, rejection, past hurt, or stronghold. I learned I didn't have to be put together to walk with Jesus—He sat with sinners. I only had to let Him do an inner work within me and he showed His power through me. We may never know why God chose us until we are delivered from what separates us from Him. Will you stay in the dark or be transformed by the light? The Holy Spirit gives me strength to continue walking in deliverance.

When I want to give up, I remember that I'm the only one in my immediate family faithfully walking with the Lord. Freedom is my portion, and I've come too far to turn back. The enemy would love to pull me into an unhealed place. Yes, I had fun in the streets, but I wasn't free—I was bound. I overcome the urge to quit this journey by remembering the Lord's goodness. There is too much love on this side to return to the other side. I'm still walking through deliverance; it is a daily process of transformation. Are you willing to let the Lord do the inner work in you every day? We all have areas the Lord wants to deliver us from. When I notice something in myself that isn't right, I take it to the Lord because I want to be changed. It's like going to a doctor for healing. At the start of my journey, I had wild faith even before fully knowing Jesus, and He showed up for me. Now, with a relationship with Him, it's easier to have greater faith, trusting that He will complete the good work in me.

Salvation changes your habits. It costs you your lifestyle and requires submission to the will of God. Many are afraid to surrender fully because they don't want to give up their old ways. I can honestly say, I'm having more joy living for Jesus than I ever did in the streets. I had big fun before, but I still felt empty inside. In Christ, I feel whole. Being a disciple of Christ isn't easy. The devil fights us the hardest because we walk in true faith with real power and authority. He doesn't fight other religions—they don't threaten his kingdom because they don't lift up the name of Jesus. As Christ believers, we are a threat to darkness. Walking with the Lord you will have to always stay alert.

Not all money is good money, especially fast money. During hard times, when the economy is bad or I'm not working, I've realized I can't chase money illegally the way I used to. That would cost me my salvation. My salvation is more valuable than anything in this world. I may not have everything I want, but I have Jesus. I may not have access to things I had in the past, but I am secure in Him. The cost of salvation can leave you empty for a while, but it's part of the process. I remind myself daily to trust God's plan. In the world, I was used to man's wicked system—I could get whatever I wanted by scamming. Now, no matter how much money I need, I will never go back to that life. I quickly decide to live out my salvation, stay free, and trust God. Even when life is hard, the Lord hears me and gives me more than anything man's system could ever offer. I get to trust Him with everything, even when I don't know where my next blessing is coming from. I just know that the more I believe, the more He shows up—even in small things.

There was a time during the pandemic when I ended up taking a car from a dealership in Woodbridge, Virginia. I didn't plan to steal it—I came with money down—but because of how things played out, I ended up on the run with the car for about eight months. This happened because the dealership messed up my paperwork after I had already signed for the car. I put down a $1,000 down payment but they tried to rip me off. Since their scam didn't work, in retaliation, I scammed them back. Since they messed up my paperwork and it wasn't financed on my credit, they wanted me to make payments to their dealership until they figured it out. However, knowing that this happened, I disregarded making payments and never contacted the dealership again. They would send me threatening text messages to bring the car back saying that they're with the mob and thought I was going to be scared. But I made sure my insurance was paid so I had some proof that the car was mine just in case they wanted to legally press charges on me. My temporary tags did expire, but since it was during the pandemic, we were allowed to drive with expired tags. I had so much fun driving a nice Infiniti off the dealership making no car payments for almost a year. It all came to an end one night when I parked in front of my house. Usually, I would park blocks away and walk to my house to hide from the dealership, but that night I was tired and just parked out front. That was the day my time on the run ended. It was a wild journey, but I truly believe it was the Lord keeping me safe.

I lived a lifestyle with the mindset that I knew how to get what I wanted, no matter the cost—even if it meant giving up my freedom. It's sad, but this is my story. It's more than a story, it was a mindset, my way of thinking, my way of surviving. Then everything changed when I met King Jesus. I learned I didn't have to live in survival mode anymore. All I had to do was fully trust in the Lord Jesus, who died on the cross for me and my sins. What does that look like now? Some days I still don't have the money to pay bills or eat what I want, but it doesn't feel like I'm in survival mode anymore. I feel safe and covered. Truthfully, I am covered by the blood of Jesus. Over the past year, I've realized that salvation comes with a safety net. Because when things in my home are falling apart, I don't feel shaken. I don't feel moved. I know that the Lord got my back beyond what I can see. *"Now Faith is the substance of things hoped for, the evidence of things not seen."* according to Hebrews 11:1.

It's still not easy, don't get me wrong, but life in the world wasn't easy either. The difference now is the safety net around me. I know I'm covered, and that feeling means more than anything the world can give. My trust in God has grown over the last two years. I've faced situations that could've pushed me to get money illegally, but choosing not to do that has strengthened my foundation in Christ. He really is my solid rock. I did so many things that could have cost me freedom, but the Lord covered me.

In 2015, when I was locked up, my faith had really grown more spending that time with God consistently showed me that He can use any situation to get glory. Those three months in jail were some of the happiest times for me. I didn't have to worry about anything—bills, problems, or daily struggles didn't matter because there was nothing I could do about them. I felt very protected. At that time, a lot of good people from my area were also locked up, and we formed a bond, keeping each other covered. The Lord used that time to minister to me and show me that He is all I need. When I came home, I had strong faith in Him, but I still didn't have a deep relationship with Him. Most of my praying was just blessing my food or asking for forgiveness. Still, my faith was strong, and I believe that's what kept me. This is why you can't give up on God—because He will never give up on you, even when you're not fully locked in with him.

The Holy Spirit spoke to me recently in my prayer closet and told me that people are dying without salvation. Knowing you may never see a friend or family member again is scary. We should want others to be with us in eternal life. Don't get too caught up in worldly desires and forget we all have somewhere to go—Heaven or Hell. So many people around me since childhood have passed away—at least 20–25 people I knew personally in my generation, mostly from gun violence. To think that could have been my life humbles me. The lifestyle I lived put me in danger. When I bought my first gun at age of 21, I walked the streets believing it would protect me. In reality, using it would have cost me my freedom or my future. My real protection came from above. The angels of the Lord kept me safe in neighborhoods and situations where I had no business being.

Growing up, my parents didn't raise me to be for the streets, but I fell in love with that lifestyle. I think it's not strange that I went down that path, because now I can go back into those dark places and bring the love of Jesus there. I used my gift for the world when it was really meant for the Lord's kingdom.

I've learned not to despise the places the Lord has put me, because one day I will go back for a God-driven purpose.

Chapter 6

SOLD OUT FOR JESUS

I would've never thought that a person like me is someone Jesus would choose. I did so many dirty things that I never imagined my life could look like this. Having 3 abortions by the age of 25, and still not learning my lesson after that because I was having unprotected sex whenever I felt like it but this time, I would pop 'Plan B—day after next' pills like they were skittles just to avoid pregnancy. Sometimes I still can't believe I'm free, because I never saw it for myself. I never knew what a minister or an evangelist was. I was a real live gangster. How can Jesus use somebody like me? I truly feel like I didn't deserve His love, but He still gave it to me anyway. There is so much freedom in being with the Lord.

Man, I've never felt so much joy without having to stop feeling joyful. What I mean by that is, in the streets, people would be so jealous of me because of my personality and looks. It would make me shut down on some days and not be who I really am or put a cap on how joyful I was so I wouldn't bother other people. Now, looking back at it, that was nothing but the enemy trying to steal my joy. Your joy will disturb dark entities. There are more dark people in this world than you think.

Coming from a world of trends, styles, comparisons, and insecure or judgmental women and men being around me, it feels good to be around a community of Kingdom women and men who want nothing but the best for me. I noticed that the world just wants to suck you dry, especially being around worldly people, but once you get around people who truly have an end goal of living for Christ in mind, it's the best thing ever. I realized that once I gave my life fully to Christ. I honestly didn't see myself living another life outside of drinking, smoking, and living on a housing voucher. I've been living on a DC housing voucher for most of my adult life. I thought my end goal was to receive a permanent voucher and be living on discounted rent, and I thought I would be winning. But when you accept Jesus, you are accepting the plans that He has for you—and I know that He has more for me regarding my living situation.

What I thought was a win for my life doesn't even compare to the wins He has for me. Since I've accepted Jesus, I've received more unusual favor. Thank You, Lord. I know it only comes from Him. He's so good to those who fully trust and love Him. Many people think they have to automatically start living a holy lifestyle to receive Jesus, but I'm here to tell you that we have a Father in Heaven who is more reasonable than that. The Lord still made plans for me while I was in my sin. I couldn't believe it. I never thought I was that worthy. But how dare you think you're not worthy when you are God's creation? He understands that we live in the world, so we are bound to make decisions and live lifestyles that are of the world and not for His Kingdom. That doesn't mean He's going to throw us away. He gives us a chance to repent and ask for forgiveness for our worldly lifestyles and decisions so we can start living for Him.

Slowly, I noticed the worldly ways and desires of mine drop away as I made the decision to grow in Christ. I didn't just stop cussing—I was still coming to church cussing up a storm. But through the strength of God, I slowly put away my foul language. Salvation is the most beautiful thing you can ever receive. It's a gift that allows you to keep living abundantly even after you die—I choose Heaven! I need you to understand that Heaven and Hell are real. Living abundantly or living miserably after death is real. The spiritual world was here long before the foundation of the world. If you don't believe me, I challenge you to ask the Lord Jesus right now to give you a sign. I say this to show that salvation is a gift that keeps you living for eternity.

"At the name of Jesus every knee shall bow,

in heaven and on earth and under the earth,

and every tongue shall confess

that Jesus Christ is Lord."

— (Philippians 2:10–11)

This scripture states that every single person on this earth will get in the posture to bow and confess the name of Jesus—even those under the earth. This shows me that Hell is real, and they too will confess the name of Jesus. So, you might as well confess it now on earth, rather than waiting until you're in Hell, when it is too late. Don't wait until it's too late to give your life to

Jesus. I thank God that He kept me while I was in the streets. He kept me long enough to come over to the light. The lifestyle I was living would've had me dead or in jail at a young age. I lived an illegal and dangerous lifestyle—there were so many things I was doing on a regular basis that could've been my downfall. God's grace sustained me while I was living a dangerous life.

I'm so glad that He found me, and that I found Him. My first love was my father, and when he died in 2009, the streets became my second love. How I made it out alive, sometimes I wonder. Now, the most important love in my life is King Jesus *(Yeshua Hamashiach)*. It was very difficult to overcome my past life, but with the strength of God, it became possible. The temptation was really the most difficult part for me—having those old feelings rise. Some days, I just want to roll up a jay (known as a "blunt") and smoke it to ease the pain. That's what I've been used to doing since I was 16. But I'm making a daily decision to stay delivered. It's all about your decision-making in the process. Are you deciding to maintain your deliverance when temptation comes, or do you give in?

If I were to give in to temptation and backslide, then all the souls depending on me and watching me walk with God would think I was playing around and not taking my walk with the Lord serious. Who knows what that would cause them to think about their own journey, or if they would even still want to follow Jesus? I know God's grace is sufficient, but to whom much is given, much is required. It's required of me to walk this thing out and withstand temptation to show people that Jesus can truly deliver you. So, follow me as I'm following Him, so you can know Him for yourself.

I'm called to the unchurched—speaking the good news to those who are living exactly the lifestyle that the Lord called me out of. I know that I may be the most Jesus they ever get. Sooner or later, I can lead them to Jesus. A lot of ministries today are purposed to edify the body of Christ, which is a great thing. But I know that my ministry is to edify the unchurched—to lead them into the body of Christ. And as I started walking closer to the Lord, the more He started to reveal my purpose.

So, I bless God that He's allowing me to write this book you're reading now, because I want you to walk your deliverance out. Continue to make the decision to stay delivered. Your reward may not come right away, but you will soon see why it was all worth it. Saying yes to God has absolutely been the hardest but best thing I've ever done for myself. The plans He has for my life are way better than anything I could've set up for myself. I was pretty much over life to a certain extent, where I was fine with just working, smoking, and drinking my life away. But once the Lord cleaned me up, He has literally been guiding my steps into righteousness and blessings.

Oh, how good it is to follow the Lord. I'm way happier and free—free from hurt, past pains and traumas, past sabotage and backstabs. I'm most importantly free from the enemy's plots and schemes. But I can say this: sometimes the enemy's plots and schemes won't harm or kill you. Instead, the Lord will turn it around for His good, and it will birth purpose out of you.

We all know that Jesus had to shed His blood on Calvary so that we could receive salvation and be forgiven for our sins. After Jesus died and rose on the third day with all power and authority, He appeared to His disciples and let them know they would receive the Holy Spirit. So not only did He shed His blood on the cross for our salvation, but this also brought forth the Holy Spirit, which is a gift from God to be our guide and helper. Judas betraying Jesus had to happen for the fulfillment of prophecy. This was a horrible situation, but beauty came out of it to help each of us, including you reading this right now. This lets me know that God ordained betrayal to come forth in Jesus' life. My question to you is, what betrayal have you gone through that pushed you into your purpose?

We serve a God who works everything out for the good of those who love Him. Not one tear is wasted. God is a redeemer of time. All that time you may feel you lost with that person or situation; the Lord will restore it. Sometimes, our next destination requires the insight gained from betrayal. Being sold out for Jesus is literally an act of stepping out in faith and obedience—not caring what the world or other people think. Be free of people's opinions. Being sold out for Jesus is really walking out your salvation. Salvation is about deliverance, surrender, relationship and holiness. When you've managed all of these, then you're truly sold out for our Lord and Savior. I'm really about my father's business.

Chapter 7

THE GODLY TRANSFORMATION

The beautiful young lady that I've turned out to be today is by the grace of God. He transformed me into ways that are still so surprising to me. My looks are different, I talk differently, and I even desire different things for my life, things that are so peaceful. Believing in the Lord has by far been the only reason I look healthier. I was starting to look like the world had beaten me up—coming outside with bonnets on, not caring how I looked because I wasn't encouraged, and losing weight due to drug intake. Just slowly letting myself go.

What made me want to fully surrender to Jesus was that I honestly had nothing else left. I had no point to live and felt no purpose in me. I wanted to find my true identity. I knew I was special but just wasn't walking in the chosen life the Lord ordained for me, and I started to feel it. I could literally feel the deadness in my spirit and my soul. I felt out of alignment. I never knew it was because I wasn't aligned with God's Spirit—I just felt like I was living to survive. I stopped smiling and stopped prioritizing my happiness on a regular basis.

I remember about six months before I got delivered, an incident happened at my door. I was selling weed and pills out of my apartment. At that time, a boy in my building owed me money from a previous weed sale, but he never paid me. I knew he was trying to run a game on me. He called me another day trying to buy more weed. Since I knew he still owed me money, I allowed him to send the money, but I kept it and did not give him the drugs he paid for. He got so angry that I "took his last bit of money" and decided to come to my door to fight me. He tried to kick my door down to the point where my door became loose. If I had lived in an older building, he surely would have kicked it down. I could hear him outside the door being extremely aggressive. However, on the other side of the door, I had grabbed my gun, my brand-new Glock, waiting for him to kick it down. I was ready to risk my life, knowing I would've been put in jail—but I didn't care. He threatened to tell me not to come out of my apartment. He didn't know that on the other side of the door, I was willing to shoot. That same night, he moved out of the building. He must have known that what he did was absolutely insane and that there could be some serious consequences. I was so relieved that he left because I didn't want to be in any more drama where I lived. I had lived a lifestyle where I constantly looked over my shoulder, so I didn't mind going to war where I lived—even though I didn't want to. But now, here I am today, able to testify that the Lord washed me clean!

It's like my past sins were forgiven, and now my past is used for His goodness. It's like He turned everything around. The streets know my track record. However, when it comes to where I'm going in my future, there's no history of my messed-up past—no history in the Spirit, that's hindering me from elevating in God. Miracles started manifesting in my life—things that I know I'm not doing on my own, but through the power of God. I can finally breathe again. I don't have to look over my shoulder when I'm out on the street anymore. I can live free, knowing that I've been released from my past sins. While people may talk about how dirty my past was, the Lord wiped it clean. Instead of my past hindering me, it's going to work for me. The Lord will place people in your life who are equally yoked to you and whom He has called you to be around. Being around the wrong people may not hurt now, but it will hurt later.

The enemy has a way of attaching himself to you by using the people around you. Knowing that I had just gotten delivered out of my old lifestyle, he trys to send a familiar spirit into my life. So always check your circle to make sure these are the folks who are authorized to be in your life. I've learned over the past two years in my journey that everything that glistens ain't gold. Make sure people respect how far you've come. If they respect how far you've come, they will cherish your life like it's their own. Many people will say they care for you, but they will be the same ones the enemy uses.

When I came off the streets, I did not drop my street smarts. Realizing that it's called discernment. Every believer should be asking the Father in Heaven for more discernment. It will save you from the enemy, who prowls around like a roaring lion, seeking whom he may devour (1 Peter 5:8).

Be careful of other spiritual sources that are not connected to Jesus—angel numbers and certain things the world uses that are not Jesus Christ. Nothing in the Bible talks about angel numbers. God has a whole book of Numbers in the Bible and does not speak about angel numbers. However, the Lord can speak in numbers, so be very discerning about how you use divine things and know when it's of God and when it's not. Be careful what you are using to connect to God, because you don't want to dabble in ungodly entities thinking it's of the Lord when it's really not. The Bible speaks against sorcery. When you engage in sorcery, you are allowing other demonic forces to come in.

I had to learn that people will use the word "spiritual", but their spiritual walk is not rooted in Jesus, and that is dangerous. Make sure you find yourself a good church home that can help you spiritually grow in the Lord. It's very important that everyone has a church home to hear the Word of God and to have a community that can walk with you. After getting delivered, I couldn't imagine only having my street friends and not knowing anyone at my church. It felt good to have a church family who understood what happened in my life supernaturally. I never even knew there were good people in my area. I mean, I knew they were there, but in my opinion, it was a rare breed in the streets. When I got to the church, I realized I didn't have to go far to find genuine people. I highly recommend that those who are tired of fake friendships to go and find a Kingdom brother or sister in Christ.

My process of transitioning from being a nightlife party and street girl into becoming a holy daughter living for the Most High has been a journey that requires patience. I had to trust the process because transformation doesn't happen overnight. Even though I received the Holy Spirit, the fruits of the Spirit had to manifest in me. I was encouraged to know I would see the fruits of my labor, and if I just stuck with this process, it would all pay off because I'm trusting in the Lord of Hosts. I am still growing and learning till this day.

I would get calls from people from my past wanting to do the activities that I no longer want to indulge in, not understanding my journey. I had to learn that carnal people will not always understand spiritual things. There was no point in getting frustrated that they didn't understand me—I knew it's hard to understand the things of God when you're living a worldly life. But I stayed faithful in the Lord by making sure I was connected to like-minded people.

Being connected to my church community really allowed me to be in an environment that led me to continue focusing on Jesus. I thank the Lord for His church. If it weren't for the church of Christ, I don't know how I would've been able to walk this deliverance out. Not every church is for everybody, you must really pray and look for signs of confirmation to know if the church you're seeking is right for you.

Being in the Lord now is way better than being in the world for the simple fact that I am free. I have joy and peace that surpass all understanding. I'm happy in the middle of chaos. I was slowly sinking when I was in the world. I had temporary happiness, and my relationships weren't as true as my Kingdom friendships. Do you want to live for a moment or for a lifetime? I've realized that worldly fun and worldly wins are momentary, but the things of God are forever—even after life. Do you want to be connected to the Creator or the creation? The world is focused on the fact that they have material things but forget that the Lord created them. When I locked in with the One who created it, I started to have way more!

"For the earth is the Lord's, and the fullness thereof."

— (Psalm 24:1)

Locking in with the Lord will unlock supernatural blessings in your life. If worldly desires please you, then by all means, do what you need to do. But there is nothing greater or more fulfilling than the divine manifestations of God. Giving your life to the Lord and surrendering it all to Him has by far been the best decision I've made, even when it became hard. The promises of the Lord are far greater than anything I could even imagine. That's why I'm deciding to stay on the Lord's side—the grass is greener on this side.

Chapter 8

DON'T JUDGE

You shouldn't judge church people, and church people shouldn't judge you. Coming into church as the "unchurched," I never felt worthy enough to be around church people. I already knew my lifestyle was too dirty to be around people who were locked in with the Lord. I thought I could never communicate with them. But the truth is, I was judging them by their outer appearance.

Now that I'm saved, I look completely different. Somebody looking at me today would probably never know I was that street girl two years ago. Now that I went from unchurched to churched, I can truly say I misjudged the people who were in Christ. I thought they wouldn't want to deal with somebody who sinned like me. But you never know where Jesus has brought somebody out of. You never know who has a worse testimony than you. You never know how somebody grew up or what strongholds GOD has delivered them from. Once Jesus cleans you up, you will not look like what you've been through. That's the redeeming power of the Lord. So, it's not good to judge a book by its cover without ever getting to know the chapters. And church people shouldn't judge the unchurched, because they don't know what promises the Lord has over their life. You may see a drug addict, but the Lord sees His child—someone who still has a promise over their life. Your job is to never judge, but to help them get free. When I was tied up in worldly desires, I never knew that all I needed was to get free through Christ.

"My people are destroyed for lack of knowledge."

— Hosea 4:6.

These people don't know that freedom is available through Jesus Christ. So, will you be the one to educate them, or will you judge them? Will you be there way of escape? You can be the answer to somebody's deliverance and breakthrough. Don't judge anyone for what they're in, knowing that the LORD is the One who brought you out. GOD spoke to me one morning and said, *"You never know who has a prayer life."* Once I realized the Lord spoke that to me, I started applying it to the world around me. You must be very careful how you treat the unchurched, because you NEVER know who is praying.

But the Lord said to Samuel, "Do not look on his appearance or on the height of his stature, because I have rejected him. For the Lord sees not as man sees: man looks on the outward appearance, but the Lord looks on the heart." (1 Samuel 16:7)

One thing I realized is that people in the church may try to downplay your value and your relationship with GOD based on how you look and how you dress. This is why Jesus came and sat with sinners in the first place. Let this be an example to you that it doesn't matter what picture the public tries to paint of you. None of your sins are too dirty for God.

I relate to Mary, His disciple, a lot, because she was a drunk. Jesus found her in her drunkenness and made her whole. Her lifestyle did not defile who she was in the Kingdom of God. Please, if I haven't told you anything else, hear me now—do not let your worldly lifestyle defile who you are in the Kingdom of God. When you meet Jesus, He will purify you from the inside out, if you let Him. It's a decision you must make. But it's a process—it doesn't happen overnight.

The Lord is so kind, because He doesn't expect us to start living holy the moment we receive Him. He knows it's a process and a daily decision. It's like getting undressed. You take your shoes off, then your socks, then your shirt—one by one. You don't rip everything off at once. There are layers you must take off. In the same way, lifestyle changes happen slowly. You take things off one by one, not all at once. Trying to take everything off at one time is impossible.

As you grow in Christ, certain behaviors and lifestyle changes happen over time. If I accidentally slip up and sin, that doesn't take away who I am in the Kingdom of GOD. But don't let this make you think you can just do whatever you want and then repent. Repentance has to come from a heart that's truly postured to do right but accidentally did wrong. I always feel like everything I've gone through in the world was to be used for a time like this. The more I endure, the more the Lord can use me for. One of the fruits of the Spirit is long-suffering. Everything I endured growing up in the streets was literally all a part of the Lord's plan. Now I'm more effective in taking back our streets from the hand of the enemy. The same streets that I used to sell pills in. Those same streets that I used to run night and day. The streets that I used to stay the night in my car to make drug sales. The same streets that showed me love and hate. I'm so glad I grew up the way I did, so I can all use this for God's Kingdom.

People don't like to suffer for long. They're always quick to get out of hardship, not realizing that hardship is what produces who we are today.

"Not only that, but we rejoice in our sufferings, knowing that suffering produces endurance, endurance produces character, and character produces hope." (Romans 5:3-4)

You never know what people are battling or how hard they had to fight to walk in freedom. Sometimes it's fun being lost. Sometimes you want to stay in that lost space because it's comfortable and it's what you're used to. What I'm living in now is freedom—it's just freedom I'm not accustomed to yet, freedom I need to get used to. That's why you can't judge or speak on whom the Lord is raising up. If you put your mouth on something that GOD has His hand on, you can end up hindering yourself.

Truthfully, we are all born gifted. The Holy Spirit determines which gifts you will have. But most of the time, we unknowingly use our gifts for the world, or we use them in another source without realizing they come from our Creator. What a joy it is to be connected to the Creator of the universe and to truly tap into the spiritual gifts placed inside each of us. Another reason not to judge is because people in the world may have a carnal mind—but that doesn't mean their mindset can't shift into a prophetic atmosphere. You won't truly know what's prophetically in you until you walk upright with the Father in Heaven.

Each gift placed in us is meant to equip the Kingdom of God. So just because someone may not be walking in their calling doesn't give you the right to judge them. Truthfully, the gift in them can be way more powerful than the gift in you. It just hasn't been activated yet!

Our job as servants of the Lord is to push people to have a relationship with the Father, no matter how they look or what they do. Focusing on deliverance wasn't the first thing that helped me—it was focusing on building a true, authentic relationship with the Lord Jesus Christ. As I started to grow in that relationship, He began removing things from my life that no longer fit my salvation. My goal for those coming to the Father is to make sure they are diligently seeking Him, building a relationship that will cultivate their Kingdom gifts. As they grow in their relationship with the Father, the Lord will deliver them from strongholds, bondage, generational curses, and more.

In the body of Christ, we cannot judge new believers who are still caught in sin, because this may be a new walk for them. It's not for us to deal directly with their sin—we have to let the Lord do His work and let the word convict them. Our job is to pray for them and encourage them. There is a certain type of grace we need to show new followers and believers of Jesus Christ. We must not judge them for what they do not yet know.

Chapter 9

THE WALK OF FAITH

"Now the Lord is the Spirit, and where the Spirit of the Lord is, there is freedom."

— (2nd Corinthians 3:17)

I'm thankful, knowing that a lot of people didn't make it out. Some are dead, some are in jail, and others never reached their full purpose in life but here I am living for the Lord. Many are blind to the fact that the Bible lets us know that a good man's steps are ordered by the Lord. God has a plan for every one of us, but we have to choose to tap into it. We will never fully know who we are until we tap into the power of Jesus Christ.

One of the keys to a successful life in Christ is humbling yourself and tithing.

"Humble yourselves before the Lord, and he will exalt you."

— (James 4:10)

I've seen Him exalt with my own eyes. When you walk in humility, you take on a Christ-like characteristic that allows the Lord to manifest Himself in your life. And when you tithe, you are tapping into the Lord's spiritual wealth system. Man's system will fail, but God's system is everlasting. If the government shuts down and you lose your job, man's system has failed you. But God will never stop providing—especially when you have seed in the ground. Being humble and tithing are gems that unlock the manifestation of the Kingdom of God in your life. As you walk out your deliverance, be sure to tap into tithing, because connecting to the Lord's spiritual wealth system is one of the keys that will ensure prosperity in your future.

When I got delivered, I noticed how certain "friends" stopped clapping for me. Some people didn't want me to get free because I was useful to them in my bondage. Think about it—I was selling drugs, drinking hard liquor, driving my car to the club or outside every night. I could financially afford my lifestyle. Of course, the leeches and those who benefited from me hated to see my deliverance coming. Once I was no longer available to pick them up, let them smoke my weed, or fund the turn-up, things changed. I was smoking back-to-back because I was selling it—most people around me couldn't afford to live like that every day. But for me, I always had a liquor bottle, and if I ate, everybody ate. I was very beneficial to the world while I was in bondage. But I'm here to say it's okay if they don't choose to deal with you anymore. They chose to sit with their demons, while I chose to get free from mine. The "lit" worldly life I once lived doesn't even compare to the life of glory the Lord has set aside for me.

I truly believe that coming from a worldly life—and not growing up in church—can make you a perfect candidate for the Kingdom. We know how to relate to the world because we've lived in it. We know how to go back into the same streets we once ran, not to participate but to spread the gospel and rescue souls that need salvation. We know how to move from the trenches to the suburbs and grab the lost souls. We understand the language, the codes/protocols, and the culture of the streets. Even though I'm cleansed in Christ, I still understand that world—because that was me. That part of my testimony doesn't disappear. Now, I use it to magnify the Lord. My life shows the streets that the grass really is greener on the other side. And it shows the community that if God did it for me, He can do it for them too.

Walk your deliverance out to the point where you are fully saved, yet still relatable to those who desire salvation. Never become so far removed that you forget where you came from, because your testimony is the bridge God uses to reach others. Once I decided to leave the streets alone and walk into who the Lord created me to be, something began to change inside of me. And when the change started happening on the inside, it began to show on the outside. As I started to see the Lord manifest in my life, I wanted more of Him.

I was amazed to discover that there is so much more to God than I ever knew. Since my parents didn't grow me up in church, I had no idea that you could go deep into the Lord. I thought once you say yes, you believe in Jesus then that was it. I had no idea there was more to it. When I realized how real the spiritual world is, I decided I would do whatever it takes to become more Christ-like. My daily walk continues to grow deeper, and it reminds me that if I keep believing and faithfully walking this out, the Lord will surely prosper me. I only want the things of God, because the world is getting played out. Once you get a taste of the goodness of God in the land of the living, you'll want more of Him. You eventually reach a place where worldly desires stop satisfying you, and your hunger for God becomes greater.

Once I started going to church in 2023, I felt the Lord working on my soul—doing a real surgery on me. He was the Master Doctor, for real. A year later, when I received deliverance at my church—after joining a church for the very first time in my life—I realized that the wholeness I had been seeking all these years came through surrendering to Jesus. And that was peace—real, true, sustaining peace.

I got tired of being tired. The peace of the Lord captured my heart, and I realized it wasn't just a feeling—it was a resting place. That peace was what I'd been searching for my whole life. I just never knew Jesus was the answer. I used to think I was finding peace by suppressing my feelings through smoking and drinking. But that was only temporary relief—and it came with a lifestyle that never produced peace. It was really a setup because when you live a worldly lifestyle, you open the door for demonic attachments—either to yourself or through the people around you. True, eternal peace is found only in Jesus. People often leave Christ because they haven't experienced a real, authentic move of Him yet—or they leave before they see His manifestations come forth. They jump ship too early, growing weary of waiting on God. The seed they sowed hasn't produced a harvest quick enough, so they forfeit it by stopping their walk. Let me tell you: never interrupt your seed. Let it grow for as long as it needs to grow, because when harvest time comes, no one can stop your garden from producing. The growing season may be long, but you will see the manifestations come to pass in the harvest season.

The walk of faith can get lonely, but I never expected a handout anyway. I was built to get it out the mud, and coming to Christ didn't change that mindset. I deeply appreciate the community in Christ that has supported me, but I also understand there will be times I must walk alone. We each have our own judgment day, and not everyone has the capacity to truly pour into what you need. Jesus is not a religion—He is a relationship. Being faithful to God, for me, looks like commitment. I committed to my worldly life for so long, and now I'm eager to walk in a new commitment—with the Lord—for a new life with Him.

Growing up, I understood the seasons of the streets. I was always ahead of the game; I walked with time—actually, I ran with time. As I consistently went to church for a year, I began to feel my time in the world running out. I just knew the Lord was preparing me for a new life in Him. The day I surrendered and received deliverance, the supernatural feeling I experienced let me know I couldn't play with the Lord anymore. I had encountered God enough to understand that it was time to really be all in. I'm so glad I'm on the Lord's side. I made it to the other side, and now I have a clearer understanding of who I was created to be.

Deliverance is a beautiful thing, and I'm praying that you walk yours out—in Jesus' name.

Chapter 10

I AM THE PROOF: *My journey from brokenness to redemption*

This chapter was inspired by the message "I Am the Proof" preached by my pastor Trina Hairston. As I reflected on that message, I realized that my own life stands as proof of God's delivering power.

When Pastor Trina preached this message on March 16th, 2025, it hit me hard because everything she said was relatable to my deliverance journey. I had just been free and delivered for a year, and I knew I had the proof of God's restoration on my life. One line from her sermon really stuck with me: *"Put your money where your testimony is."* It showed me that the Lord can make your story work for you.

I am proof that God can set you free, heal, and deliver. He can restore a broken mindset and mend a hurt heart. He can redeem years that I once thought were wasted. God is more than just the Lord—He is a Father and a Friend. He can lift you out of low places and seat you in heavenly places.

I am proof that He can take you out of environments filled with jealousy and place you in a community of people who love Him—and love you for who you are.

I am proof that He can plan my future, and it will be far better than anything I could have imagined.

I am proof that He can save me—from death, from jail, from the enemy's traps.

I am proof that he can redeem me from deceitful relationships, and from devastating family trauma.

I am proof that He orders a good man's steps.

I am proof that if you cry out, He will answer. If you speak to Him, He will speak back. And if you give Him your time, He will change your life.

I am proof that He can choose someone off the streets and transform them into who He created them to be.

Thank You, God, that my past is never too hard for You.

Conclusion

This book shares the testimony of Kayla Crawford—how she was once on a pathway leading to destruction and is now on a journey toward her promised land. Her journey can be compared to the Apostle Paul on the road to Damascus. Paul was heading toward destruction when Jesus met him, changing his life forever and repurposing him for the ministry God had planned.

Paul faced hardships and went through a season of blindness, where scales were lifted from his eyes, giving him new vision and a new identity. Similarly, while Kayla was heading down a path of destruction, an encounter with the Father transformed her life. Even through hardships, every step was part of God's process to prepare her for His plan.

Her story is a reminder that God can meet anyone on their path, lift the scales from their eyes, and guide them into the destiny He has prepared. No matter the journey, transformation is possible when we surrender to Him.

No matter how far you've strayed, God can meet you on your path, give you new vision, and lead you into the life He has always intended for you.

www.ingramcontent.com/pod-product-compliance
Lightning Source LLC
LaVergne TN
LVHW042344150826
845671LV00001B/14

* 9 7 9 8 2 3 4 0 1 6 5 6 0 *